PAPISTS
PROTESTING

Againſt

𝔓𝔯𝔬𝔱𝔢𝔰𝔱𝔞𝔫𝔱 𝔓𝔬𝔭𝔢𝔯𝔶.

I N

Anſwer to a Diſcourſe Entituled,
A Papiſt not Miſ-repreſented by Proteſtants.

BEING A

VINDICATION

Of the

Papiſt Miſ-repreſented and *Repreſented*,
And the *Reflections* upon the Anſwer.

LONDON,
Printed by *Hen. Hills*, Printer to the King's moſt Excellent
Majeſty, for his Houſhold and Chappel. 1686.

PAPISTS PROTESTING

AGAINST

𝕻𝖗𝖔𝖙𝖊𝖘𝖙𝖆𝖓𝖙=𝕻𝖔𝖕𝖊𝖗𝖞.

MY *Replier* begins with Complements; and I cannot but admire his art of weaving raillery into them so neatly, that every Eye will not discern which is which. But of all his Complements I take the *Reply* it self to be the greatest. Now in good manners I should take my turn with my compliments: but am forc'd to drop these, and stand upon my guard; for the *Replier*, while he Compliments me with one hand, is giving me a box with the other; in his very next lines calling in question my *honesty*, without any mincing it at all. In the Misrepresentation of a Papist, he says, *I have shew'd some Art, but very little Honesty.* The *Replier* said just before that he would *compliment no more*, and is as good as his word. As for me, I am much mistaken, if I find not upon occasion, more vouchers for my honesty, then Art: If I did by chance stumble into it, 'twas against my inclination, and I am sure I fell up-hill.

But he would have my Art lye in this; that whereas I was told in the *Answer, that some of those misrepresentations, which I had made of a Papist, and*

p. 1.

A 2 *given.*

given out for the Protestant Character of Popery, were
my own ignorant, or childish, or willful Mistakes, I
craftily insinuate, that they grant all my *Mis-repre-
sentations of a Papist, to be ignorant, childish, or willful Mistakes. Which is in short the Answer gives
some, and I take all. And yet those two little words,
upon which the whole Stress and Truth of his charge
lie, are neither in the Answer nor Reflections; but
are providentially juggled in here by himself, to give
the Reader an early taft of his own Honesty, while
he challenges mine. The Answerer had said, must
the Character now suppos'd to be common to Protestants,
be taken from his ignorant, &c. Mistakes? The Reflecter says, Because you say my Character is made up
of false apprehensions, ignorant, &c. Mistakes. What
difference is here in fense at all? And what difference
even in words; fave that I add false apprehensions,
which the Answerer likewise has in the very next
page? Neither of us mention all or some, which the
Replyer, not without reafon, fufpects of craft. As
the Answerer thereof meant, I aflure him, I meant ;
the whole Character, if he meant fo ; and part only,
if he meant no more : Nor did I ever think of ex-
tending his Authority farther than he extended it
himfelf. If the Replyer find any Att in this, I for
my part, find no difhonefty ; and think I have ill
luck to fall into his bad opinion, for keeping precifely
to my Adverfaries fenfe, and almoft precifely to his
words.

The Replyer comes after this with full Cry, and
asks, what is the meaning of all this pother and noife
about this double Character of a Papist Mif-reprefented and Reprefented ? Truely I cannot tell, and think
he would do well to ask those who make it ; for they
in

in all likely-hood know beft. I for my part thought it a very inoffenfive thing, to let people know what *Papifts* are, and pray God there be not a fear they fhould appear what they are, leaft they be found to be unlike what they are made appear. They have been cry'd out upon, for keeping the people in Ignorance of their Doctrines; and when they expofe them to open view, 'tis ftrange there fhould be a noife about it. Truly I did not expect it, and I could not imagine a bare Narrative of matter of Fact fhould fructifie into *Anfwers*, and *Reflections*, and *Replies*. I did but relate, playing the Hiftorian, not the Controvertift : Not but that, with the liberty of Hiftorians, who deliver their own judgment of the matters they relate, and their reafons for it, I difcover'd what I thought, and fometimes faid briefly why : But every Body will fee, I made not Difputing my bufinefs. And yet, I know not how, it is taken it feems, for a piece of Controverfie, and which is more unreafonable, againft the *Church of England*, and defences made for her, as if my *Mif-reprefented Papift*, were a *Reprefented Church of England Proteftant* : Whenas I never gave that Character out for a *Church of England* Character of *Popery*, thought nothing of her Rule or Judgement, nor dreamt of concerning her, or any Body in my Mif-reprefentation, whofe Confcience do's not of it felf concern them. All thofe, who have fuch Idea's of us, as I there draw, I faid Mif-reprefent us ; and to thofe who have not, I faid nothing. He that would know whether he be concern'd or no, has but to ask his own Heart, to which I did then, and do ftill leave him.

And yet notwithftanding this harmlefs juftifying our felves, there is a *pother* and *noife* it feems about
the

the *Papiſt Miſ-repreſented and Repreſented*, and it is
as fiercely aſſaulted on every ſide, as if it came to
declare open war, and bid defiance to the world. The
Anſwerer ſet upon it in the *Miſ-repeſenting* part, and
will have that to be *falſe apprehenſions* of the Author,
to be *taken from his ignorant, Childiſh or Wilful mi-
ſtakes* : And then the *Papiſt Repreſented* he endeavours to overthrow with whole vollies of Objections. Now comes the *Replier*, and tho he makes it
wonderful hard (*p.* 40.) to know what the Faith of
a Papiſt is; yet he acknowledges it in the ſame page
to be true, as the Repreſenter has declar'd it, excepting ſome few points; and therefore paſſing by
the *Papiſt Repreſented* with ſome light touches only,
his main attack is againſt the *Papiſt Miſ-repreſented:*
and not being willing this ſhould be underſtood, as
p. 3. if made up of Childiſh, Ignorant or Wilful Mi-
ſtakes, he will have it to be the very avow'd Doctrine and Practice of the *Church of Rome.* He will
have the *Papiſt Miſ-repreſented and Repreſented* to be
all the ſame, excepting ſome very few caſes.

And this he has urg'd ſo far, that I think, 'tis not
now ſo much my Perſonal concern, to make an *Anſwer*, as the concern of as many as throughout the
whole World profeſs themſelves *Catholicks*, to con-
ſider the truth of what is here charg'd againſt them.
The Salvation of their Souls, their Eternity is at
ſtake. If what is here poſitively aſſerted againſt them
be true, 'tis high time for them to reform, and to leave
off the Doctrine and Practice of ſo much Heatheniſm,
under a Chriſtian Name. *Proteſtants* in hopes of a
mutual condeſcendence, may flatter them as they
pleaſe, and tell them, they have Charity enough to
think they may be ſaved ; for my part I declare, if
Popery

Popery be guilty of what he fays, it cannot enter into my thoughts, there's any room for it in Heaven:
and that there's any more poffibility of a paffage for
its monftrous extravagancies through the *Narrow*
way, then for thofe of *Barbary* and *Turky*. The *Po-*
pery, this Author defcribes,feems to me a flat Contra-
diction to the Commandments and the Gofpel; and
the Profeffors of it can have no other portion then
with Idolaters, Murderers and Adulterers, whofe E-
ternity is to be in utter darknefs.

He declares plainly that *Popery* is really that *An-*
tichriftian Religion, which *Proteftants* fay it is; that
it teaches and practices all thofe Fopperies, Superfti-
tions, and Non-fence, which have been at any time
charg'd againft it by *Proteftants*. His very Title of
A Papift not Mif-reprefented by Proteftants, is a con-
demnation of the Religion to all thofe horrid fhapes
and monftrous forms, it has been at any time expos'd
in by Members of the Reformation. He tells his
Reader in the name of all his Brethren, *We charge*   p. 4.
them (the Papifts) *with nothing, but what they ex-*
prefly profefs to believe, and what they practice: And
in this one Affertion vouches for the Truth of all that
Infamy, and prophanefs which is laid at their doors.
And fo gives affurance, that their complaint of being
Mif-reprefented is but vain and idle; for that, what
they call a *Mif-reprefentation*, is in reality a *Repre-*
fentation in all the material Points, of the avow'd Doct-   p. 2. 3.
rine and Practice of the Church of Rome. That the *Pa-*
pift Reprefented (excepting fome very few cafes)
profeffes to believe all that the *Papift Mif-reprefented*
is charg'd with. This, *the beft and wifeft Men*, he
fays (*viz.* of the Reformation) *have believ'd of them.*   p. 2.
And in Fox's *book of Martyrs we read how many were*
                                                        burnt

burnt for not believing, as the Papist Mis-represented believes. This is the General Character of a *Papist* according to the freshest and most Modern draught of our *Adversary*; So that now to receive a true information of the *Papist's Creed*, we are not to consult the Council of *Trent*, or the Catechism *ad Parochos*, but the writings and Sermons of *Protestants*: For however *Papists* may not know what they believe themselves; yet *Protestants* give a true and exact account of them, and are so far Infallible, that the *Papists* certainly are, what they say they are; believe what they say they believe, since *they charge them with nothing, but what they expresly profess to believe, and what they practice.* Upon the assurance of this *Affidavit*, me-thinks, 'twill not be amiss here to receive the satisfaction of knowing, what a *Papist* really is, and what he certainly believes, beyond the possibility of all exception. For since all that proceeds from a Popish hand of this nature, is suspected and challeng'd, and the *double Character of a Papist Mis-represented and Represented* (about which, as the *Repliers* says, there is so *much pother and noise*) is questioned as to its Method, its Sincerity and exactness, we'l now follow our Authors call, and learn what *Popery* is, from the Pens of *Protestants*: and especially from some of those, who are supposed to know what *Popery* is; but for the *bad man*, which the *Replier* excepts against, we'l make no advantage of him, but let a better Man take his room.

What

What Papifts are according to the Character given by the moft Reverend Father *John* fometime Lord Archbifhop of *York,* in his Book Written for the ufe of a Lady, to preferve her from the danger of Popery, where he brings in a Papift thus declaring the Belief and Doctrine of his Church.

*W*E *muft Believe the Church of* Rome, *whether it teach true or falfe.*

If the Pope Believe there is no Life to come, we muft Believe it as an Article of our Faith.

We teach that the Gofpel is but a Fable of Chrift.

That the Pope can difpence against the New Teftament, that he may check when he pleafes, the Epiftles of St. Paul, *and controul any thing avouched by all the Apoftles.*

That there is an eternal Gofpel, to wit, that of the Holy Ghoft, which puts down Chrifts.

That Chrift is the Saviour of Men only, but of no Women: For Women are faved by St. Clare *and Mother* Jane.

That we put away Mortal fins, by becoming Francifcans, by a Bifhops Pardon for Forty days, and a Cardinals for a Hundred, and the Popes for Ever.

That to become a Monk or a Nun, is as good as the Sacrament of Baptifm.

That Whoredom is allowed all the Year long, and another fin for June, July, Auguft, *which you muft not know: Allowed for this time by* Sixtus Quartus *to all the Family of the Cardinals of St.* Lucie. B *That*

That the Pope can make that Righteous, which is Unrighteous.

That the Bishop of Rome *is a God.*

That the Pope may dispence with all Duties, and that our Principles set Men loose from all obligations in all relations whatsoever, between Magistrates and Subjects, Lords and Tenants, Husbands and Wives, Parents and Children, Masters and Servants, Buyers and Sellers.

That there is not any sin, but is or may be Indulged amongst us ; and scarce a known sin, but there is a known price for it, and at our Market-rate you may commit them when you will.

What is the Belief and Doctrine of the Papists, as 'tis deliver'd by *Tho. Beard* D.D. in his Book Entituled, *Antichrist the Pope of Rome.*

THey *Believe that Saints departed ought to be Worshipped and invocated with trust and confidence as God himself.*

That the Pope can Canonize them to this Worship at his pleasure.

That Images are to be adored with the same degree of honour as is due to their Patterns, contrary to an express precept of the Law.

That the Pardon of sins here in this Life, and deliverance out of Purgatory in the Life to come, may be bought for Mony, and where no Mony there no remission.

They make their unwritten Traditions, not one, but the principal part of Gods word

They

*They place divers counterfeit Books, disguised under
the Name of some of the Apostles, or their Disciples,
full of Fables, Blasphemies, and Contrarieties, and
yet commend them to the World as parcels of the written word of God, and Believe in them as Holy Scripture it self, as the Gospels of St.* Nicodemus, *of
St.* Thomas, &c.

*The Pope hath set up a new God in the Church, namely
a piece of Bread in the Mass——and to their Bread-
en-God they ascribe power to forgive sins, to defend from
evil both Men and Beast, and to bring to Heaven——
when as in the mean while most horrible Blasphemies
against Christ himself are tolerated and slighted over.*

*The Pope is above Angels and Magistrates, he ex-
alteth himself above all that is called God, yea, above
God himself.*

*They prefer their Saints before Christ : They rely
more upon the mediation and intercession of Saints, then
upon the mediation of Christ.*

They not only equal St. Francis *and St.* Dominick
*unto Christ, but in some things prefer them before
him.*

They affirm that whoever dies in St. Francis's *habit
cannot be Damn'd, and that it is as forcible for the
remission of sins as the Sacrament of Baptism.*

What the Papists are as Represented by Mr. Sutcliffe in his *Survey of Popery.*

*T*Here *is no point almost, wherein the Papist vary
not from the antient Church, the Article concerning the holy Trinity only excepted.*

B 2   *They*

They teach novelties and false Doctrines concerning the very grounds of Faith ; for they believe the Church to be built upon the Pope.

They speak what they can, in disgrace of the holy Scripture.

They give the Office of Christ's mediation to the Virgin Mary, to Angels and to Saints, they make also Saints our Redeemers &c.

For God they Worship Creatures, not only giving divine honour to the Sacrament, but also to Crucifixes and Images of the Trinity made of Wood &c. and they do adore not only Saints, but rotten bones and rags, they know not of whom.

They overthrow grace and ascribe the merit of our salvation, not to God's mercy through Christ, nor to the merit of his passion, but properly to our own works and merits.

They cut out the Second commandment, because it cannot stand with the Popish worship of Images.

They pray before Stocks and Stones, nay they put their trust in them.

They make no conscience to cut Christian mens throats for not yielding to all their abominations, and think it conscience to obey the Popes decrees, tho very unlawful.

The Fourth commandment concerneth the sanctifying the Sabbath, but the Papists profane it by Worshiping Idols, and frequenting the Idolatrous Mass.

Papists think they do God good service when they murder true Christians.

Amongst Papists , Adultery and Fornication are reckoned among lesser sins.

By the Doctrine of Papists the Devils of Hell may be saved——To this purpose they say, that not only wick-

ed and reprobate men, but also the Devils of Hell may have true and justifying Faith.

Papists blasphemously make Christ not only a desperate Man without hope, but also an infidel without Faith.

They deny Christ to be αυτοΘεὸς, and affirming that his divine Essence had a beginning from some other, they fall within the Compass of the errour of the Tritheites, which Herasie doth tear the Unity of the Godhead in pieces, and plainly makes more Gods then one.

Papists do diminish the merit of Christ's satisfaction, and enervate, as much as in them lieth, the Cross of Christ, and the effect of his death and passion——They are teachers of Antichrist, opposite to Christ, and enemies of his Cross.

That Christ is not the redeemer of all Man-kind.

They make Christ inferiour to Saints and Angels, and prefer the Pope before Christ.

Papists make St. Francis and Dominick, equal to Christ in divers things, and in some things Superiour.

They give equal honour to a Cross of Wood and Metal, and to Christ, and looking on a Wooden crucifix they say, thou haft redeem'd us.

They suppose the Virgin Mary more merciful then Christ.

Papists account it a small sin to use common Women.

Papists believe divers were by their Saints fetch'd out of Hell.

Papists by their irregular Doctrines and Traditions, have not only corrupted, but also difanul'd; for the most part, the law of God.

They deny the Gospel to be a rule of perfection, but they doubt not to give that honour to the rules of Bennet, &c. they speak more Blasphemously of the Holy Scriptures, then the Turks or Saracens.

To

To the Images of the Cross and crucifix, they give as much honour as they do to God.

They fall down like Beasts before the Pope, and Worship him as God, ascribing to him most blasphemously the honour due to Christ.

Popery as a sink, hath together with Heresie receiv'd into it self most gross and Heathenish Idolatry.

Papists say they put no trust in Images, but never did the Gentiles trust so much in the Images of Juno, or Jupiter, as the Papists trust in the Images of our Lady of Loretto, James of Compostella, &c.

They give divine honour to Images, which they themselves cannot deny to be Idolatrous.

They ascribe mans justification to his Works, and exclude justification, both by Christ's justice, and by Faith, &c.

The Papists teach their disciples to distrust Gods grace———and to trust rather in their own Works and Merits.

Popery is nothing else, but a pack of old and new Heresies.

Papists despise marriage as Pollutions and fleshly life.

Bennet, Dominick, Francis and other authors of feigned religions took not their Rules from the Gospel, but thought they could frame a more perfect religion then the Gospel.

As the Gentiles had one principal God, and divers demy and inferior Gods, so have the Papists.

As the Gentiles believed that every one had his good and bad Genius, so the Papists assign to every Christian a good and bad Angel.

The second Council of Arles cap. 23. sheweth it to be a custom of Pagans, to worship Trees or Stones, or
Fountaines,

Fountains, yet our *English Papists* cease not to go on pilgrimage to *St.* Winifrides *well*, nor to worship Stocks and Stones.

The *Romish Church* consists of a pack of *Infidels*. They forbid honest *Wedlock*.

The *Papist Preachers* seldom teach the people, and when they do it, they preach their own inventions, and tell idle tales without edification.

Both *Priests and People* are most ignorant of Matters of Faith, where *Popery* is profes'd.

The Scriptures and Fathers they read not.

In a member of the *Catholick Church*, (they say) neither inward *Faith* nor other *vertue* is requir'd, but only that he profess outwardly the *Romish Religion*, and be subject to the *Pope*.

The *Papists* promise *Heaven* to their followers, so they profess and set forward the *Popes* cause, whether they be *Murderers of Kings*, or *Massacrers*, or *Rebels*, or filthy *Whoremongers*, or *Sodomites*.

They make more conscience to abstain from flesh on Friday, then to murder *Christians*.

Divers points of *Popish* doctrine are specially said to proceed from the *Devil*.

It is a common practice amongst *Papists* to give divine Worship to dead men.

The *Popish Church* hath no true *Bishops*.

The *Pope* is *Antichrist*.

The *Popish Synagogue* hath no true *Priests*.

Popery in many points is more absurd and abominable, then the doctrine of Mahomet.

Papists, that positively hold the heretical and false doctrines of the modern *Church* of Rome, can not possibly be saved.

What

What Papifts are according to the Book of Homilies.

Images in Churches and Idolatry go always both together——Images in Churches have been, be, and ever will be none other but abominable Idols.

Oenomaus and Heſiod ſhew that in their time, there were Thirty thouſand Gods; I think we had no fewer Saints to whom we gave the honour due to God, and they have not only ſpoiled the true living God of his due honour in Temples, Cities, &c. by ſuch devices and inventions that the Gentile Idolaters have done before them, but the Sea and Waters have as well ſpecial Saints with them, as they had Gods with the Gentiles, &c.

Papifts make of true Servants of God, falſe Gods, and attribute to them the power and honour which is Gods, and due to him only.

Image maintainers have the ſame opinion of Saints, which the Gentiles had of their falſe Gods.

Image maintainers Worſhip Stocks and Stones, they give alſo the honour due to God to their Images, even as did the gentile Idolaters to their Idols.

Who can doubt but that our Image maintainers agreeing in all Idolatrous opinions, agree alſo with them in committing moſt abominable Idolatry?

In many points our Image maintainers have exceeded the Gentile Idolaters in all wickedneſs, fooliſhneſs, and madneſs, and if this be not ſufficient to prove them Image-Worſhipers, that is to ſay, Idolaters, Lo you ſhall hear &c.

The Learned and Unlearned, Laity and Clergy, all Ages, Sects and Degrees of Men, and Women, and Children of whole Chriſtendome have been at once drown'd in abominable Idolatry, the ſpace of Eight hundred years and more.　　　　　　　　　　　　　　This

This is the *Protestant Character* of a *Papist*, and such as I always look'd upon no other, than of a Papist *Mis-represented*; and whoever will take the pains to compare it, with what I set down under that Title, will find there's little other difference between them, but that this is the *Fouler*. But now it seems it must be no longer a *Papist Mis-represented*, but *Represented*, and 'tis what the *Best and Wisest Men have Believ'd of them*. And here now what shall I say? Our *Replier* says, these are *Great and Good Authorities*, and we may well suppose they knew what *Popery* was. And for my part because I love not quarrelling, I shall so far joyn with them; that if *this* be the *Popery* they have hitherto prosecuted with so much Fervour and Zeal; if *this* be the *Popery*, from whose infection they have so industriously Laboured to deliver the Christian World, they have done nothing but what is the *duty* of every true Believer. And if 'twas for the not Embracing *this Popery*, those Martyrs Recorded by *Fox* pass'd the Fiery Trial, their Cause was surely a Glorious Cause; and I question not the Triumphs and Crowns of Glory that waited for them in Heaven, were not inferior to what those enjoy'd, who suffer'd under *Decius* or *Dioclesian*. And for my part I am so far in earnest, had I a Thousand lives, I would rather choose by the assistance of Heaven, to loose them all at the *Stake*, than in the least assent to so much Heathenism, to so Foul and Monstrous a Religion. And what need now of any longer disagreement? What necessity of keeping up Names of Division? *Protestant* and *Papist* may now shake hands, and by one Subscription close into a Body, and joyn in a fair and amiable correspondence. *Popery* has been hitherto the only

C   cause

cause of Separation; one part seeming to avow and support it, the other as Zealously endeavouring its overthrow. And all the strife it seems has been about a *Word*. For now we have been inform'd from *Great and Good Authorities*, what this *Popery* is; what Papist in the World is there, that will not so far become *Protestant*, as to give his hand for the utter suppressing *this kind* of *Popery*? And when *Protestants* and *Papists* concur for the rooting out of *Popery*, what possibility of Farther Divisions?

But if on the other side, *this Character* of a *Papist* be intended, for the setting forth the Doctrines and Practices of the Church of *Rome*; if this be design'd as a *True Representation* of the Faith and Religion of *Roman Catholicks*: Then returns afresh my complaint of their being *Mis-represented*; that they suffer under the greatest injustice imaginable; that they are expos'd in *Bears* and *Tigers* Skins, so to become a Bugbear to the Multitude: That they are malign'd and render'd odious for the maintaining such Doctrines, which they as heartily Detest, as those that urge the charge; and that 'tis no wonder that *Papists* are put in the List with *Turks* and *Infidels*, since their Religion is thus injuriously loaded with Calumnies, and they made the Professors of such Tenets, which bid open defiance to Truth, Honesty, and Christianity, which strike at the Worlds Redeemer, and are impossible to be entertain'd by any Creature, that is one degree above a Beast.

I will not deny, but whosoever will look into the Church of *Rome*, as the *Scavanger* does into the City, who stops no where but at a Dunghil, may rake together so much as to defame her with the Inconsiderate and Unwary; alas the Vices of Men in her Communion,

munion, their abufes of the moft Sacred things, too
abundantly furnifh matter of this kind. But yet
whofoever fhall expofe this for the Doctrine and
Practife of their Church, and defcribe her, and all
in her Communion by thefe Rubbifh Collections, cannot poffibly avoid the fcandal of being unjuft, and
might with as good reafon decipher *London* by thofe
loathfome heaps where all her filth is emptied. And
now fince 'tis evident, the Adverfaries of the Church
of *Rome* do generally thus deal by her, fcraping out
of every corner of that vaft Communion and in every
Age, whatfoever can poffibly contribute to make her
infamous ; there is too too much reafon to complain
of her being *Mif-reprefented,* and no juft exception
can be made againft the Character of the *Papift Mif-
reprefented,* which lays open to the World the Ar-
tifice of thefe unwarrantable proceedings.

But here now ftrikes in the *Replyer,* who undertakes to explain a Myftery in this Character ; and the
Reflecter, he fays, *will have no reafon to glory, that
he gave the occafion of it.* And this Myftery it feems, p. 3.
are fome faults he has difcover'd in the *Mif-reprefentation.*

1ft. He fays fuch things are put into this Character
of a *Papift,* as *no Man in his wits ever charg'd them
with :* And yet thofe very things almoft in exprefs
terms, and others far more abfur'd, we fee charg'd
(as is fhew'd above) *by the Beft and Wifeft of Men,*
of great and good Authority with the *Replyer,* as he
confeffes himfelf. (*p.* 2.) And this too is to me a
Myftery as well as to him ; that what no Man in
his wits ever urg'd, and what the former *Anfwerer*
calls *Childifh,* and *Ignorant,* or *Willful miftakes* fhould
be now feen Father'd upon Men of fo high a Character.

2ly. And

2*ly*. and 3*ly*. He complains, that the Opinions of *Protestants*, and the consequences they draw from Popish Doctrines, are put into the Character of a *Papist Mis-represented*, as if they were his avow'd Doctrine and Belief. This is a pretty speculative quarrel, I confess, and might deservedly find room here, were it our business to consider the due method of *Mis-representation* in the *abstract :* But as our present concern stands, here's a quaint conceit lost, for coming in a wrong place. For what had the Author of the *Papist Mis-represented* to do with these Rules? He did not intend to Mis-represent any body. His Province was only to draw forth the Character of a *Papist*, as 'tis commonly apprehended by the Vulgar, or the Multitude, with the common prejudices and mistakes that generally attend such a notion. Now I would fain know, whether this Character, as it lies in the peoples heads, is distinguish'd into *Antecedents* and *Consequents :* Whether they, when they hear one declaiming against Popery, *for committing Idolatry, as bad or worse than that of the grossest Heathens, Worshipping Stocks and Stones for God,* distinguish between the *Doctrine* of the *Papists*, and these *Interpretations* and *Consequences* charg'd against it. Alas they swallow all down greedily and in the lump; *Antecedents* and *Consequents* go down with them all at once. Neither do I find much care us'd to prevent this misunderstanding in the People. For who is there in laying open the folly, as they will have it, of the *Papists*, and positively charging them, that *They make Gods of Stocks and Stones,* that *They make Gods of dead Men, and raise the Virgin* Mary *to be co-partner with Christ in Heaven,* &c. Does afterwards tell his Auditory, that This is not what the
Papists

Papifts themfelves *Believe* and *Teach*; but only what himfelf *Believes* and *Infers* from their Doctrine, as the *Confequence* or *Interpretation* of it, but they deny.

Truly were our Adverfaries fo fincere as to tell their hearers, that all their charge againft *Popery* is nothing more, than what they *think* of our Faith and Doctrine; I would fo far agree with the *Replier*, that this ought not be call'd Mif-reprefenting, but only faying of us, what is not true. But they go beyond this, and inftead of faying *we think fo*, they pofitively fay *fo it is*: And poffefs as many as take Ideas from their words, not barely that they think we Teach and Practice Idolatry, *v. g.* but abfolutely, that we do. Nay our Image-worfhip, is Worfhiping Stocks and Stones for Gods, fays the *Replier* in his very next leaf without remembring his *thinking*.

And when the People read Books, intended as *prefervatives* againft the danger of *Popery*, they are ftill expos'd to the like deceit. For what ordinary Reader is there, that finds it pofitively afferted as above by the Arch-bifhop of *York*. *Papifts Believe the Church of Rome, whether it teach true or falfe. And if the Pope Believes there is no Life to come, they muft Believe it, as an Article of their Faith*. What ordinary Reader, I fay, is there, that will not fwallow this prefently as the *Faith* and *Doctrine* of the *Papifts*; when at latter end 'tis only what he *thinks*, and a *Confequence* far fetch'd to difcredit *Popery* with the Vulgar? And when he's told by another hand, that the Common Anfwer of *Catholicks* to excufe themfelves from Idolatry *in their adoration of the Eucharift*, is becaufe they *Believe the Bread to be God*: Has not he here a fair occafion again of taking this for the *Belief* of a Papift; and that he Worfhips, what he

Believes

Believes to be a *Breaden God*? Certainly he muſt be no ſmall *Logician* that can diſcover, whether this be an *Antecedent* or *Conſequent*, whether it be the *Faith* of the *Papiſt*, or only a *Conſequence* of it. For my part, when I ſee *Popery* deſcrib'd, as if none could be of that Communion, but he *that can bring his mind to Believe the Word of God to be writ but for a few Tears only, and afterwards to be abrogated and annull'd. That whatſoever God ſays, ſhall be null and void, unleſs the Biſhop of* Rome, *will and command the ſame.* When I hear that the *Pope* is Antichriſt, and *Rome* the Whore of *Babylon,* that *the Papiſts have taken away from the People the Holy Communion, the Word of God, the true Worſhip of the Deity, the right uſe of the Sacraments and Prayers, and inſtead of them, have given to pleaſe them, Salt, water, Oyl, Spittle, Bulls, Jubilees, Indulgences, Croſſes, Incenſe and an infinite number of meer Toys and Baubles, and that in theſe they have placed all Religion;* when I hear, I ſay *Popery* thus deſcrib'd to the People by eminent Apologizers for the Church of *England,* I cannot conceive, but 'tis to let them know, what notion to frame of it. And yet whoſoever ſhall ſuppoſe, that after ſuch directions, they'l conceive a regular Idea of it, without a confuſion of Faith with its *Interpretations,* of *Doctrine* with its *charges,* muſt conclude them to be better at *Separating* than the *Chymiſts,* and that in ſubtle *diſtinctions* they are able to outdo *Ariſtotle* himſelf. But 'tis too much to be fear'd, that thoſe who expoſe *Popery* to the People after this way, are not willing they ſhould apprehend it in its genuine Purity, and as free from this diſingenuous mixture: 'Tis ſo like thoſe who impoſe upon the Multitude with artificial Monſters, by putting the wrong end forward,

ward, and shewing the Tail for the Head; that if they are not deluded into a mistake, 'tis because they are not so credulous as they should be, and suspect something of a Trick in him that makes the shew.

And has not the *Reflecter* now reason to repent after all, that he gave occasion to the *Replier* of explaining the Mysteries, he has discover'd in the Character of the *Papist Mis-represented*; since the faults he endeavours to lay open, are not in the Mis-representation, but in those, who by Mis-representing the Papist, rais'd a false Idea of Popery in the Peoples heads? The Character of the *Papist Mis-represented*, was intended only, as the Author expresses himself in his Introduction, for a *Copy* of Popery as Painted in the Imagination of the Vulgar: And being conform to that, 'tis exact and perfect : And if there be any faults in it, the blame must fall on those who drew the *Original*. But however we'l compound here again for this ; if the *Replier* will but undertake to undeceive the People, and give them a more exact Notion of Popery, the *Reflecter* will undertake to reform the Character accordingly. But till then the Character of the *Papist Mis-represented* stands good; and till the abus'd people are taught to distinguish between *Antecedents* and *Consequents*, between the *Faith* of *Papists* and the *Consequences* charg'd against it; the Character must remain as it is ; and any Reformation in it would but make it Irregular, and unlike that from whence it was taken. The *Replier* therefore might very well have spar'd the almost Forty pages he has spent on this Subject; in which, tho he has learnedly distinguish'd between matters of Dispute and of Representation : Yet this distinction being not to be found in the Notion the People have of Popery,

'tis

'tis nothing to our purpose. And the only end it can possibly serve for, is to let the World understand, how much the Papists are generally wrong'd in their reputation; whilst so many grosse absurdities, which are often positively expos'd for Articles of their Faith, are here acknowledg'd by the *Replier* himself, not to be their *Faith*, but only the Interpretations and *Consequential charges* of their Adversaries.

These are the *Mis-representing* Arts and Faults he mentions. For the *Representing* Faults he alledges. 1. *That I deny the Belief of their Interpretations.* And the reason is, it may be, because he thinks, no body charges us with *that Belief*: Which if it be but true, then I have not so much as contradicted any body, and there is no fault, I hope, in that. 2. *I generally own the Doctrines and Practices, which they charge us with.* And how could this possibly be otherwise, if they charge us with none, but what we expresly profess to own? 3. *That in some cases I disown that to be the Doctrine and Belief of our Church, which manifestly is so and has been prov'd on them.* Then for all his word to the contrary, we are in some cases charg'd with more than we expresly profess to Believe. As for his *manifestly*, and his *proving*, let that go for no more than what it is, his Opinion: 'Tis none of mine, and I think 'twill be no bodies else, when the matter comes to a Trial.

And here now we must turn over so many Leaves, till we meet with some other matter in the *Reply*. And the first that occurs, are some exceptions against the Rule observ'd by the *Representer* in declaring the Faith of a Papist, who to clear himself from the Scandal of Interpreting the Council of *Trent* by his own private sense and opinion, alledges the

Cate-

Catechifm ad Parochos, which he had follow'd in delivering the fenfe of the *Council.* This the *Replier* could not pafs by without an Anfwer, and therefore gives a fatisfactory one. *And is he fure,* fays he, *that all his Reprefentations are conformable to the fenfe of this Catechifm? May he not play tricks with the Catechifm, and expound that by a private Spirit, as well as the Council?* Thus a Queftion or two is a full Confutation of the *Reflecter.*

He alledg'd again the Bifhop of *Condom's Expofition of the Doctrine of the Catholick Church,* which being approv'd and attefted by the *Pope* himfelf, by feveral Cardinals and Bifhops, brought along with it the Authority of the *See Apoftolick.* But this it feems, works nothing upon the *Replier: Canus* has put a fcruple in his head; and becaufe he finds in this Author, that *That is not to be accounted the judgment of the Apoftolick See, which is given only by the Bifhop of* Rome *privately, malicioufly,* (a word flipt over by the *Replier*) *and inconfiderately, or with the advice only of fome few of his own mind;* he cannot therefore think, but that the Bifhop of *Condom's Expofition* comes fhort of the Authority of the *Apoftolick See;* and that the *Reflecter* is out, in taking fhelter under one, whofe *Authority is nothing,* as he fays down-right, *pag.* 46.

This is Anfwering I confefs with a witnefs, thus to endeavour to overthrow fo confiderable and Reverend an Authority, without any Authority at all, befides that of an ungrounded and ill-turn'd confequence; *viz.* Becaufe that is not to be accounted the Judgment of the Apoftolick See, which is given only by the Pope, *privately, malicioufly, and inconfiderately, or with the advice only of fome few of his own mind;* there-

therefore this Learned Prelate's *Expofition of the Catholick Faith* is to be thrown by, as of no Authority. So that our *Replier*, has here concluded without any more adoe, that the approbation of this Book was only given *privately, malicioufly, inconfiderately,* or elfe with the advice only of fome few of the Popes own mind, otherwife the Confequence will not hold. But to fhew how little the *Replier* has weighed this matter, and with how little pains he can undervalue any thing when he pleafes: I need only remit the Reader to the perufal of the Book it felf, which is lately publifhed in Englifh; the *Advertifements* affixt to it will fatisfie him, that there has not a Book appear'd in this Age fupported by greater Authority than This. He'l find it examin'd with all due deliberation, approv'd with all folennity imaginable, by Men of known Integrity, Piety and Learning, by Abbots, Cardinals, Bifhops, and by this prefent Pope himfelf, and recommended by his *Holinefs* to be Read by all the Faithful. He'l find it not only thus approv'd, but even twice Printed at *Rome* it felf, and in the Prefs of the Congregation *de Propaganda Fide*, Tranflated out of the Original French, into divers Languages, as *Latin, Italian, Englifh, Irifh, Flemifh, High-Dutch*, and this done by eminent Men of thefe Nations: So that befides the Atteftations of thofe great Men there fpecified, it may be faid to have the General Approbation of all thefe Catholick Prelates, who in propofing it to their Flock, fufficiently recommend it for a True Expofition of the Doctrine of the Catholick Church. And yet notwithftanding all this, with the *Replier*, it has not the Authority of the *Apoftolick See*; nay its *Authority is juft nothing*.

Now

Now methinks, I would willingly here know of the *Replier*, whether Those *Great and Good Autho-rities* above mention'd, who pretend to make a Survey of the Faith and Doctrines of *Catholicks*, have better Authority and Grounds for what they assert and charge, than this Reverend Prelate for the Exposition which he gives. And whether it be not a great Mystery, that every *Divine* of the Reformation shall be thought to have Authority sufficient, for defaming the Church of *Rome*, with whatsoever extravagant Opinions he can but find in one or two Writers of what condition soever: And yet a *Catholick Prelate*, Eminent in the Church for his great Vertue and Learning, in expounding the Faith of his Church, with the Consent, Approbation, and Authority of the Greatest Men of his Communion, and even of his Supream Pastor, shall be slighted, and thrown by as of *no Authority* at all. For my part I cannot understand this uneven kind of justice, and reasoning: Or why those who profess a Religion, and depend on it as to their Salvation, shall be thought less to understand it, than others who protest against it, and look no farther into't, than to render it Ridiculous. But it must be so in an Age, in which a *Papist* is not to pass for a Christian, and must not be believ'd; we'l therefore go on to the other points.

And for the clearing the most material of them, we need not look beyond the Exposition deliver'd by this *Prelate*.

1*st*. As to the *Invocation of Saints* he declares expresly, that They have no other capacity of assisting us, *but only by their Prayers*. And tho the *Replier* pretends, there's no such limitation found in this Author; yet methinks he should not have been so positive,

pofitive, in a cafe, in which he's fo eafily difprov'd.
The French Edition Printed at *Paris* 1681. has it
exprefly, *pag.* 32. The Firft Englifh Edition Printed
likewife in *Paris* 1672. *pag.* 29. And now this laft
Correct Edition, which came forth the laft Week,
pag. 9. So that, tho the *Anfwerer* has made fome
little objection; yet the *Reprefenter* is fufficiently
vindicated, in thus declaring the Faith of a Papift:
fince what he faid, is founded not upon his own private fenfe, but upon an Authority beyond all exception, befides that of meer *Cavil.*

3*ly.* And 3*ly.* As to the *Papes perfonal Infallibility,*
and the *Depofing Power*, the *Reprefenter* declar'd, that,
tho there were Men of his Communion maintaining
thefe Points by way of *Opinion*, yet that they were
no part of the *Catholick Faith*; and that *Papifts* had
no obligation from their *Church* of affenting to fuch
Doctrines. And for thus delivering a matter of *Fact,*
he has the Authority again of this Great *Prelate,*
who having declar'd the *Primacy* of St. *Peter,* and
acknowledg'd the fame in his Succeffors in the See
of *Rome*, immediately adds: *As for thofe things,*
New Edit.
P. 50.
which we know are difputed of in the Schools, tho the
Minifters continually alledge them to render this Power
odious, it is not neceffary we fpeak of them here, feeing
they are not Articles of the Catholick Faith. It is
fufficient we acknowledge a Head eftablifh'd by God to
conduct his whole Flock in his Paths, which thofe, who
love Concord amongft Brethren, and Ecclefiaftical
Unanimity, will moft willingly acknowledge.

And is not this a fufficient difcharge of the *Re-*
prefenter from all the exceptions of his Adverfaries?
For if this learned Author, having propos'd the Primacy of St. *Peters Chair* to be acknowledg'd as the
common

common Center of all Catholick Union, do's pur-
pofely wave all other Points relating to the Authority of that *Chair*, as being *no part of the Catholick
Faith* : And his Book in this form is own'd and approv'd by the *Pope* himfelf, by the moft eminent of
the Cardinals, and other great Prelates of the Churh
after a moft ftrict examination, what ground of quarrel with the *Reprefenter* in his following this fo Authentick a Rule ? 'Twas the main defign of the Bifhop
of *Condom* in that Treatife to feparate the opinions
of Divines and School Debates, from the Doctrine
of the Catholick Faith. And fince he omitted to
expound thofe Points of the Popes *Perfonal Infallibility* and the *Depofing Power* as not belonging to the
Catholick Faith, with fo full and Authentick an approbation, as has been declared ; where is the crime
of the *Reprefenter* in not allowing them a place in
that Lift?

  And here I cannot but run the venture of another
fmile from the *Replier*, upon the reinforcement of
my former Propofal. I defir'd that the decifion
of the quarrel with the *Reprefenter* might depend upon the experiment of any ones being judg'd capable
of being receiv'd into the Catholick Church, upon
his affenting to matters of *Faith*, in that form
as deliver'd by the *Reprefenter*. The *Replier*, having
fmil'd firft, thought it not fit to put it to that iffue;
but chofe rather to own that the Faith, as declar'd by
the *Reprefenter*, was really the Faith of *Papift*, excepting the *Depofing Doctrine*, and fome other few
Points. Here then let him make the Propofed Trial,
if he pleafes, or any friend for him; and if, notwithftanding his refufal to admit the *Depofing Doctrine*
and the *Popes Infallibility*, but as Stated by the
                                                   Repre-

p. 40.

presenter (that is, not as Articles of Catholick Faith)
he be not judg'd sufficiently qualified as to those
points, to be receiv'd into the Communion of the
Roman Catholicks, I will grant he has reason to
charge the *Representer* not to have done his part in
those Particulars. This will be a much shorter and
surer Conviction then twenty *Answers* and *Replies*,
fit only to cast a mist before the Readers eyes, and
which such a tryal as this will quickly dissipate.

And this now is all that is requisite for a full Vindication of the *Representer*. For it being franckly
own'd by the *Replier* himself, that he has made a
true Representation of the *Faith* of a *Papist*; with
the exception only of some few Points. And it being here made evident, that what the *Representer* deliver'd as to those very Points, is according to the
sense of the *See Apostolick*, of the greatest Prelates,
nay, I may say of the whole Church : *The Papist
Mis-represented and Represented*, stands untouch'd.
And all that has been laid against it, have been nothing more, then so many artificial endeavours to
perswade the World, that the *Protestant* understands
better, what the *Faith* of a *Papist* is, then the *Papist*
do's himself ; which will be easily answer'd after his
manner, with a smile.

What the *Replier* adds after this, belongs not to
the *Representer*, who being to *Represent*; and not
to *Dispute*, is not concern'd with those tedious arguments ; however, not to be uncivil, we'l go so
far with him, tho it be out of our way.

1. He proves at large that all *Definitions of Faith*,
declar'd in General Councils are not concluded with
Anathema's; and in this we willingly agree with him :
But this do's not at all prove, that whatsoever is

declar'd

declar'd in such a Council without an *Anathema*, is an Article of Faith ; and therefore nothing against us deserving any farther answer.

2. He endeavours to prove the *Deposing Power* not to be a matter of *Discipline* and *Government*, but to be a Point of *Doctrine*, and this from a Principle lately published in the vindication of Dr. *Sherlock's* Sermon, viz. that *To decree what shall be done, includs a virtual definition of that Doctrine on which that Decree is founded.* And this he says, *as we have been lately told.* But what respect can I possibly have for what has been lately told us by another hand, since the *Replier* himself, however he urges it in one page, plainly undervalues it and contradicts it in his very next ; where he tells us, that in the Council of the Apostles at *Jerusalem* there was a *Decree of Manners*, yet *it contain'd no Definition of Faith*. And for my part I think the *Replier* in the right, and must needs stand with him against the *Vindicator* of the Sermon; that *to decree what shall be done, do's not include a virtual Definition of Doctrine.* And the example produc'd by the *Replier* evidently shews it : For tho the Apostles in their Council (Acts 15.) decreed *abstinence from blood and strangl'd meats* : Yet this Decree of *what was to be done*, did not include a *virtual Definition of that Doctrine, on which the Decree was founded* : For if it had, then the *Doctrine of abstaining from blood and strangled meats*, had been an *Article of Faith*; which I am sure is not agreeable either to the Principles or Practices of either of our Churches. And the reason of this may be, because Decrees of *what shall be done*, are often made with relation to particular circumstances, of *time, persons, place,* &c. and not built upon Definitions

of

p. 53.

p. 55.

of *Faith*, but upon Prudential Motives, upon Probable Opinions, upon the Teſtimonies and Informations of Men; and ſo may be ſuſpended or quite abrogated, as alſo confirm'd a new, or wholly chang'd, according to the alteration of Circumſtances: Nothing of all which can ſtand with Articles of *Faith*, which being the indiſpenſable Doctrine of *Jeſus Chriſt*, are not ſubject to change or alteration.

p. 54.

3. But ſuppoſe this Decree to be rank'd only among the *Decreta Morum*, which concern only the Diſcipline and Government of the Church, yet our Adverſary here urges out of *Canus* and *Bellarmine*, that General Councils cannot err even in ſuch Decrees, when they relate to things neceſſary to Salvation, and concern the whole Church. And when the *Replier* has prov'd the *Depoſing Decree* to be of this Nature, and eſteem'd as ſuch by our Church, he may then deſerve a farther conſideration.

What the Replier adds of this Subject (*p. 57.*) That the *Pope* permits the poſitive Aſſertors of the *no-Depoſing Power* to paſs without any Cenſure of Hereſie, becauſe he *wants Power to do it*, is ſpoke like an *Oracle* I confeſs; but becauſe theſe are ceas'd now a days, we may very well ſuſpend our aſſent, till we have ſome better Argument, than his bare aſſurance of what the Pope *would do* if he had Power.

p. 63.

The Laſt Argument, is concerning the *veneration of Images*. And tho the *Anſwerer* was willing, without any more ado, to condemn the Papiſts of *Conſtructive Idolatry* from ſome external Acts of Adoration us'd before Images: Yet our *Replier* readily grants, that thoſe Actions are in themſelves *indifferent and capable of being paid to God and Men*, and to be us'd as the expreſſions either of a *Civil* or a *Religious* Honour.

Honour. But he has given us an infallible Mark, by which to diftinguifh between *Civil* and *Religious* Honour, notwithftanding the very *fame External Actions* being us'd in both; and 'tis, that *Civil relates to this World*, and *Religious to the Invifible Inhabitants of the next*. This he fays is a diftinction allow'd by all the reft of Mankind; and though *by all the reft* he feems willing to exclude me, yet fince he has given his word for it, I'le come in for one of that number, at leaft fo far as to fuppofe it. So that here we have it now laid down as a Principle by common agreement, that *External Actions of Honour* paid to things relating to this World, is a *Civil Honour, Refpect, Veneration or Worfhip*. And when they are paid to things relating to the invifible Inhabitants of the next, 'tis a *Religious Honour, Refpect, Veneration, or Worfhip*. And hence 'tis concluded by him, that thefe *External Acts* of Honour exprefs'd to any *Image*, that has Relation to fome Invifible Being, muft of neceffity be a *Religious* Honour. This is what the *Replier* proves, and we at prefent agree to. But if he thinks, as he fays, that this *puts an end to the Difpute*, I think him miftaken, we being as yet only in the beginning. For tho it hence follows that Papifts give a *Religious* Honour to Holy Images, yet till it be proved that *all Religious* Refpect and Honour, is *fo a Divine Honour, as* to make a *God* of the thing to which it is paid, at leaft *conftructively*; he has not concluded Papifts to be Idolaters, or guilty of conftructive Idolatry; which is the thing he intended and undertook. And that he cannot poffibly prove it from thefe Principles, without proving *too much*, and bringing himfelf in for a fhare, I think may eafily be made appear.

p. 66.

For

For if Papifts muft be condemn'd of this conftructive Idolatry, becaufe they ufe *External Acts of Adoration* to an Image, which has a Relation to fome invifible Being: muft not all thofe come into the fame Lift, who ufe the like *External Acts of Adoration* to other things, which have a like Relation to the fame invifible Being? What excufe fhall there be for him, who *Bows* to the *Altar*, or *Communion Table*, to the Name of *Jefus*, &c. All thefe things Relate to the invifible Inhabitants of the next World, and all External Acts exprefs'd to them muft by confequence be a *Religious Worfhip*: then, in the words of our *Replier, If to Worfhip any Invifible Being, he to give Divine Honours to it; then to be fure, to Worfhip the thing Relating to fuch an Invifible Being, muft be Religious Worfhip alfo. For if the Worfhip be refer'd to that Invifible Being, which the thing relates to, it cannot be Civil but Religious Honour;* and whofoever gives *Religious Honour* to a thing, do's immediately afcribe Divinity to the object of that Worfhip, and in our *Repliers* Phrafe, by *conftruction of Fact* is an Idolater.

p. 67.

And now how many here are included in this confequence? Certainly as many as admit of any Religious Refpect befides to God: Which yet the *Replier* himfelf was not unwilling (*p.* 60.) to give to Reliques, allowing a *due Veneration and Religious Decency to the Bodies of Saints and Martyrs:* And the Learned Dr. *Stillingfleet* is well enough difpos'd to acknowledge a *Reverence and Religious Refpect* due to Sacred Places and Things. So that I believe the *Replier* has overfhot himfelf in this Argument: And that upon confideration, he will admit of fome *Degrees* in *Religious*, as well as in *Civil* Honour: And that every thing

Def. p. 862. fol.

thing is not immediately set up for a *God*, which is Honoured with a Religious Respect, however this Honour may be ultimately terminated in God.

And this thought now brings into my mind, a close piece of Arguing us'd by the *Replier*, in urging this matter; and it lies thus : (*p.* 66.) *Civil Respects are confin'd to this World* ; But *we have no intercourse with the other World, but what is Religious* ; Therefore *as the different kinds and degrees of Civil Honour are distinguisht by the sight of the Object, to which they are paid, tho the External Acts are the same :* So (says he) *the most certain mark of distinction between Civil and Religious Worship is this, that the one relates to this World, the other to the invisible Inhabitants of the next.* Here we have a *Consequence* and a *Comparison*, and both so excellent in their kinds, that if any better connexion can be found in them, than betwixt the *Monument* and the *May-pole*, it must be by one, who has found one trick more in *Logick*, then ever *Aristotle* knew. If instead of his *So* in the end of his *Conclusion*, he had made this application, *So are the different kinds and degrees of Religious Honour distinguisht by the Intention of the Givers, or by some visible representation, or determination of other circumstances.* This might have been infer'd with some dependance on the Premises : And by it we might have compounded for the matter in hand : but as the *Replier* has it, it neither proves, nor is any thing.

Another Argument we have just before this, which proves again *too much*, and is so unlucky as not to harm us, without cutting the Throat of his own Cause : The force of it may be thus exprefs'd : *No intention can alter the nature of Actions, which are*

deter-

determin'd by a *Divine* or *Humane Law*; Therefore since the *External Acts* of *kneeling* or *bowing* to or before an *Image*, are determinately forbidden by the *Divine Law*, the *intention* of doing no *evil* in them, cannot excuse them from *Sin*. For do's not this as severely strike at the *Bowing down* to the *Altar*, and *Kneeling* to the *Sacrament* as at us ? For those very *Actions* are part of the *Divine Worship*, and *Bowing down* is the very *Idolatrous* Action expresly forbid in the Commandment: And then, *If there be any such thing*, (as the Replier says here) *as External and Visible Idolatry, it must consist in External and Visible Actions; for we can never know what Mens intentions are, but by their Actions; and then* (says he) *if Men do such Actions as are Idolatrous, how can the intention excuse them from Idolatry?* So that by this way of reasoning he can never throw us down, but we must fall *both together*. For tho the *Sacrament*, or the *Altar* are not express'd in the Commandment; yet since the *External Action of Adoration* is a *Religious and Divine Worship* (according to the Repliers Principle before establish'd) the *Bowing down* and *Kneeling* to them cannot be excus'd from the guilt of *Constructive Idolatry*. And whatsoever hole the *Replier* can possibly find, to get out at with his *Altar*, the *Representer* will easily follow him at the same with his *Image*.

But that the *Replier* may see, how far his Argument concludes, I would fain know whether a *Quaker* might not as reasonably make use of the same, for the justifying his *Tea's* and his *Nay's*, and his other points of *Quakerism*? For if he should say; *No intention can alter the Nature of Actions, which are determin'd by a Divine or Humane Law: But Swear not at all, Neither*

Mat. 5. 24.
Mat. 23. 10.

he

be ye called Masters, and *let your Communication be*   Mat. 5. 37.
Yea, Yea, Nay, Nay, are Actions or things determined
by the Divine Law : Therefore the *Intention of doing
no Evil in them* cannot excuse the doing otherwise
then is there determin'd, from the guilt of sin. This has
equal force from a *Quaker* as from a *Replier*, and
makes evident, that the same Arguments which per-
suade to a *Reformation* from *Popery*, do upon the
same grounds plead still for a *farther Reformation.*

Thus far have I follow'd the *Replier* beyond my
business of *Representing*, and I hope I have so far
oblig'd him in it, that however he has Question'd
my *Honesty*, he will not at last, now call me *Uncivil.*
Before I take my leave, I will be so free as to offer
him a Request or two, which will not be thought
unreasonable, I hope, since he himself has put them
into my Mouth.

1. That he will use his interest with *Protestants*, to
hold to what he says they do, and charge us with nothing, but what we expresly Profess to Believe and
Practice.

2. That they pick not up the Abuses of some, the
Vices and Cruelties of others, the odd Opinions
of particular Authors, and hold these forth for the
Doctrine and *Practice* of our Church. And that in
charging any Practices, they charge them upon no
more then are concern'd.

3. That as often as they tell what they think of
our *Doctrines* and *Practices*, They would likewise
at the same time inform their Hearers, that those
Thoughts are, as the Replier says, *Opinions, Interpretations* and *Consequences*, of their own, concerning our Doctrine, and not our *avow'd Doctrine* : But
that we think as ill of those Crimes which they
charge,

charge, as they themselves do; and that We, our
Doctrine and Practices, are as free from them, as
They think of their own; and that in *this* consists
the Difference betwixt us.

These are but very Reasonable Requests, I think,
and what every Man may very well expect from his
Christian Neighbour; they being not so much Fa-
vours as Duties: And what every one, who understands that Golden Rule, of *Doing as they would be
done by,* will comply with without long entreaties.
This is desir'd by those of the Reformation too, who
require in their Synod of *Dort,* that *None judge of the
Faith of their Churches, from Calumnies pick'd up here
and there, or passages of Particular Authors, which
are often falsly cited, or wrested to a sence contrary to
their Intention: But from the Confessions of Faith of
their Churches, and from the Declaratation of their Or-
thodox Doctrine unanimously made in that Synod.* And
this is a caution of so great importance, that where 'tis
not observ'd, 'tis no wonder to see Men contending
for the Truth of Christianity, and to lose it amidst
their Uncharitable Dissentions.

'Twas my intention not to increase, but to diminish these heats, and for this end I put forth the double
Character of a *Papist Mis-represented and Represented.*
'Twas this was the design of the Bishop of *Condom*
in his *Exposition of the Faith of the Catholick Church,*
and of the Clergy of *France,* in the *Acts of the General Assembly* lately publish'd. The method is in-
offensive, and free from provoking Reflections; and
if by this I have let the World know what our
Church Believes and *Teaches,* 'tis what I intended:
And as for Disputing I leave that to such, who think
it worth their while.

F I N I S.

Conel. Syn.

REFLECTIONS

Upon the

ANSWER

To the PAPIST

𝕸𝖎𝖘=𝖗𝖊𝖕𝖗𝖊𝖘𝖊𝖓𝖙𝖊𝖉, &𝖈.

Directed to the

ANSWERER.

SIR, I have perus'd your *Aufwer*, and am glad to find it fo moderate and calm : You make here and there fome *Perfonal* reflections indeed; but this being done foberly, without heat and paffion, I am ftill bound to thank you, if not on my particular, yet on the Publick fcore; For having by this convinc'd the world, that men of different judgments may now treat of matters of Controverfie, without making ufe of Satyr and Scurrility, or letting Cavil fill up the place of Judgment and Reafon. This method I cannot but approve as moft agreeable to Chriftianity ; And if I purfue the fame, in giving a farther explication of fome moft material Points, you have been pleas'd to queftion in my fmall Treatife, as alfo in letting you know my farther fence of Yours; I hope it may be

A   done

done without offence, and that the shortness I shall
use, will be easily pardon'd, if it be but to the purpose.

, Sir, You let me know, my First Character of a
Papist Mif-reprefented is not satisfactory, as not sound-
ed on the sense of a Party, and the quotations of Authors, but being rather my own *Falfe Apprehenfions,*
my ignorant, my childish, or willful Miftakes. Indeed
had I been bred up in a Wood, and jumpt forth into
the World, with *this Character* in my head, I should
have had reason to subscribe to you: But because, upon examination, I find I was educated in a
well-peopled Town, at the foot of the Pulpit, and
liv'd always in Company and Conversation, I cannot
imagin this Character *fo my own,* as you seem to underftand it, but rather *my own, as I receiv'd it.* And
you need not wonder that I did not heretofore by the
help of *Books* or *Friends,* receive better information,
and correct my *falfe Apprehenfions* of *Popery.* For
indeed, were I even at *this time* to be rul'd by the
greateft number of these, the Character of a *Papift*
would be with me much blacker yet, than I have
there drawn it. There would be, but few strokes of
reason of Chriftianity in it, But *Beaft* and *Barbarous*
all over. And pray do you see, Sir, what weighty
proofs are urg'd againft me, to shew how *foul* and *mon-*
ftrous a Religion I have chosen. They shew me the
Book of Homilies laying a good Foundation, Mr.
Fox's Book of Martyrs, Bishop *Ridly's* Writings,
The Publick *Teft,* A Manual of Three small Trea-
tises, by *John* late Arch-Bishop of *York*, for the
use of a Lady, to preferve her from the danger of
Popery. Printed *London* 1672. Then a large Def-
cription given by Mr. *Sutcliffe* in his *Survey of*
Popery,

Anfwer pag. 10, 11.

pag. 11.

To. 2. p. 46. 54. 213. &c.
Vol. 3. p. 515.

Popery, where he undertakes to draw its several features; as (*chap.* 10.) *That Popery is a sink of Heathenish Idolatry.* (*chap.* 27.) *That 'tis a most absurd and foolish Religion.* (*chap.* 32.) *That it is a Doctrine of Devils.* (*chap.* 47.) *That in many points 'tis more absurd and abominable than the Doctrine of Mahomet.* Then the *Anatomy of Popery* Printed at *London* 1673. in which an Argument is shown between pag. 181. *Paganism* and *Popery* in Six and twenty Points; and with the *Jews* and *Pharisees* in other *ten.* Then Mr. *Julian Johnson* who has again set forth This Compari- pag. 99. son of *Popery* and *Paganism*, especially as to *Politheism* and *Idolatry*; With the approbation of his *Answerer Jovian*, who assures him that *He, with all the rest that have so thundred of late with the Thebean Legion,* like it well, and *are as well satisfied with it*, as he him- Jov. Introd. *self is , bating some irreverent Phrases.* Nor Sir, pag. 4. amidst these *Authentick* proofs, besides a great number of other *Authors*, who undertake to draw *Popery* in its *own Colours*; what convenience or even possibility had I, of framing any better apprehension of *this Religion*, than was here laid before me: Especially since my friends were not wanting to vouch the truth of all this, and to assure me ; they had heard all this over and over from Men of *Character*, and in *Places*, which gave it reputation beyond all question? Neither does it appear to me, had it been my fortune to have consulted you in this affair, that I should have been much rectified as to these my *Childish* or *Wilful Mistakes* concerning *Popery*; as is evident from the Character you give of it throughout your *Answer*, and especially at the end (*pag.* 161.) *viz.* "That it is "that you can never yield to, without betraying the "truth, renouncing your senses and Reason, wound-

A 2 "ing

"ing your Confcience, difhonouring God, and his
" Holy Word and Sacraments; perverting the doct-
" rine of the Gofpel, as to Chrift's fatisfaction, Inter-
" ceffion and Remiffion of fins; depriving the People
" of the means of Salvation, which God himfelf hath
" appointed, and the Primitive Church obferv'd, and
" damning thofe for whom Chrift died.

But however I will not infift upon this point; He
rather yeild, than be contentious: And becaufe you
fay, that my Character of a *Papift Mif-reprefented*,
is made up of *Falfe Apprehenfions, Ignorant, Childifh and Wilful Miftakes*, Ile own it to be no better :
But then, Sir, you muft give me leave to make ufe of
your *Authority* with my Friends and Acquaintance,
in affuring them, that wherefoever they fhall for the
future either *bear*, or *read* fuch things charg'd upon
the *Papifts*, they muft give it no credit, and efteem
it no better, than the *Falfe Apprehenfions, Ignorant,
Childifh and Wilful Miftakes* of the Relatours. Upon
this condition I clofe this point ; only adding, that
in laying down the Colours of a *Papift Mif-reprefented*, I never thought of declaring the Articles of
your *Church*; or by *Mif-reprefenting* the *Papift*, to
reprefent you ; as you feem to miftake me : But only
to fhew the many *Miftakes* and *Errours* to be found
amongft *Proteftants* of what kind foever, concerning the notion of *Popery*, for *Debitor fum fapientibus
& Infipientibus*. And tho you feem willing in your
Introduction, that your Reader fhould efteem this our
complaint of being bafely *Mif-reprefented*, no better
than a meer *Pretence*, or *a Defign of fuch who go about
to deceive*, by comparing it with the Complaints of
the *Arians, Pelagians, Neftorians*, &c, Yet we are
beholding to you foon after; when finding fome of
the

pag. 9.

pag. 7.

pag. 9.

the *dirt thrown at us*, to fall upon *your own Face*, by your standing so *near us*, you then own it to be *grounded*, and *Real, pitying the Weakness and Folly of* those who Cast it (pag. 10.) And therefore I believe you will close with me in this Point, that Mif-reprefenting is Mif-reprefenting, tho from thofe who diffent from your Church. But we go on to the other Character of the *Popift reprefented*.

And this too, it feems, affords you as little fatisfaction, as the former, on feveral accounts. And Firft you move a Scruple by the by, (*pag. 9.*) by your having no mind to ask, *How the Council of Trent fhould come to be the Rule and Meafure of Doctrine to any here, where it was never received?* As if *in this Character* I had obferv'd a *Rule*, which ought to be none *Here*, nor is own'd as *Such*. And as to this, I need only Inform you ; that the Council of *Trent* is receiv'd here and all the Catholick World over, as to all its *Definitions of Faith* ; altho it be not wholly receiv'd in fome places, as to its other *Decrees*, which relate only to *Difcipline*. And therefore in appealing to *this Council*, for the vindicating all I have *there* afferted, to be the Doctrine of *Catholicks* , I have done nothing but what I was oblig'd, and is juftifiable before the whole World : and on the truth of what I have faid concerning the *Councils* being univerfally receiv'd as to Doctrines of Faith, I'le allow the whole Caufe between us to depend. But this only as to your *miftake*.

Now fuppofing this to be the *Rule* of fuch Points of Faith, as are there fet down for the Belief of the *Papifts*, you raife your Difficulty (*pag.* 11.) becaufe *I fhew no Authority I have to Interpret that Rule in my own fenfe :* it being a thing exprefly forbidden by *Pius.*

Pius 4th. And becaufe feveral of my *Reprefentations depend upon my own private Senfe and Opinion.* Truly Sir, had I, in undertaking to ftate the Belief of our Church, Interpreted the Council of *Trent* in my own private Sence, or Obtruded any Opinion of mine for an Article of our Faith, you might juftly have Arraigned me at that Barr. But you muft give me leave here to tell you, that you Wrong me, and Impofe upon your Reader. For fo far was I from committing this Fault of Interpreting the Council of *Trent* in my *own Senfe* : That I have only deliver'd it, as it is Interpreted to me and to all our *Church*, in the *Catechifm ad Parochos*, compofed and fet forth by Order of the *faid Council* and *Pius* 5th. for the Inftruction of the *Faithful* in their Chriftian Duty touching *Faith* and *Good Manners*, in conformity to the Senfe of the *Council*. And for this reafon in my *Conclufion*, I appeal'd to this *Catechifm*, for the juftifying of what I have reprefented to be the *Faith* of the *Papifts*, to be *really fo.* And that you may fee, how vainly you have charged me with the Tranfgreffion of *Pope Pius's Bull* : Remember I appeal'd again in *my Conclufion to* Veron's *Rule of Faith*, and to that fet forth by the *Bifhop of Condom*, for maintaining the Character of the *Papift Reprefented*, to be *juft.* Now you muft know the Latter of thefe, drew up a like Character in *Paris*, of the *Belief* of a *Papift*, and it being conform to the Principles of *Piety* and *Chriftianity*, it quite overthrew the foul charge of its Adverfaries *There*, from their Books and Pulpits; and this fo home, that they had no other way of preferving their Credit with their Flock, than to declare to them, that the *Character* fet forth by the *Bifhop* was not *Exact* and *True* ; but only
ly

pag. 122.

pag. 10.

ly vampt up by him into that Form for the bene-
fit of the Publick caufe. Upon which he Publifhed
another Edition with feveral diftinct atteftations of
many *Bifhops* and *Cardinals*, and of the prefent *Pope*
himfelf, wherein they at large approve the Doctrine
contain'd in that Treatife, for the *Faith* and *Doctrine*
of the *Church of Rome*, and conform to the Council
of *Trent*. And now Sir, in propofing the *Faith* of
our Church, as I found it deliver'd by this Reverend
Prelate, and fupported by fuch Authentick approba-
tions, wherein have I Entrenched upon the Priviledge
of the *Apoftolick See*, of Interpreting the Council
of *Trent ?* Or what neceffity of relying upon a *private Mans Judgement*, as you Phrafe it, *of no Name,
and no Authority*, inftead of that of the Pope and
Council ? The Faith of a Papift I have deliver'd according to the Catechifm Publifh'd by Order of the
Council, or as Explicated by a *Prelate*, who brings
along with him the Authority of the *See Apoftolick*;
and which part of all this is my *private Senfe or Opinion* ?

But you offer to make good this charge in fome In-
ftances. As in the *Invocation of Saints*, I feem to limit their Power of helping us to *Prayers only*, which
Limitation is not to be found in the Council of *Trent*.
I cannot but acknowledge, Sir, that the *Council* mentions their *Aid* and *Affiftance*, which we may reafon-
ably expect. But there being no other means of their
Aiding and Affifting us exprefs'd in the Council, or
in the *Catechifm ad Parochos*, befides that of their
Prayers to God to obtain benefits for us, through
our only Saviour and Redeemer Jefus Chrift. And it
being thus *limited* by the Bifhop of *Condom* on this
Subject (pag. 33. Edit. *Pa.* 1681.) with the *Pope*
and

pag. 272.

and *Cardinal's* approbation ; I think I need no farther vindication to shew, that in the proposal of that
Point, I follow'd not my own *private sense* or *Opinion*, as you endeavour to prove.

In the Point of *Merit* you urge this again (pag. 56.)
as if I had *qualified this Doctrine with the dependance on
Grace, on God's goodness and Promise*, without the
Authority of the *Council*; there being no such qualifi-
cation exprefs'd in *Can.* 32. read and cited by you.
'Tis true, 'tis not in this *Canon*. But if you pleafe to
look back to *Can.* 26. *Sex.* 6. you'l find it there clear
enough to aquit me from the fcandal of publifhing my
own *private fenfe* or *Opinion.*

You inftance again (pag. 11.) in the Point of the
Popes perfonal Infallibility, which I reprefent to be
no matter of Faith : (pag. 42.) and what reafon have
you, you fay, to adhere to my reprefentation, rather than to that of many others, who affert the contrary ? But this difficulty is nothing but your miftake : for I do not in the leaft deliver here my own
private fentiment or opinion touching this point, in
oppofition to other Authors : But I only by way of
Narative relate, that whereas fome Divines endeavour in their School debates to prove and maintain
this *Perfonal Infallibility*, yet it is not receiv'd a-
mongft *Catholicks* as any *matter of Faith*, becaufe not
pofitively determin'd by any *General Council*, and propos'd to the Faithful to be embrac'd as *fuch*. And this
Sir again is not my private fenfe or Opinion, but a
bare Narative of matter of *Fact.*

But I am now to encounter your *Goliath*-Argument,
which fhews it felf throughout your *Anfwer*, and
feems to defy all the Hofts of *Ifrael*. If I can find never a Stone to fling at it, I muft e'en lie at its mercy.
                                                      And

And it appears thus. In my Character of a *Papist* pag. 12. 143.
Represented I pretend to declare the *Faith* of a Roman
Catholick, as 'tis defin'd and deliver'd in allow'd
General Councils ; and yet tho the *Deposing Doctrine*
has been as evidently declar'd in such Councils,
as ever *Purgatory* and *Transubstantiation* were in that
of *Trent*, yet still *with me 'tis no Article of our Faith*.
This is the main strength of it, as urg'd by you on
several occasions.

I answer it in short ; that tho all *Doctrinal Points*
defin'd in any *approv'd General Council*, and propos'd to the Faithful to be receiv'd under an *Anathema*, are with us so many *Articles of Faith*, and are
obligatory to all of our Communion: Yet not so of
every *other matter* declar'd in such a Council : There
being many things treated of, and resolv'd on in such
an Assembly, which concern not the Faith of the
Church, but only some matter of *Discipline*, Govern-
ment, or other more particular Affair. And *these
Constitutions* or *Decrees* are not absolutely Obligatory, as is evident even in the Council of *Trent*, as is
before hinted ; whose Decrees of *Doctrine* are as much
acknowledg'd here by Catholicks in *England* and
Germany, as within the Walls of *Rome* it self, or the
Vatican : And yet it's *other Constitutions* and *Decrees*
are not universally receiv'd, and it may be never will.
Now Sir, altho we allow some Councils have made
decrees for deposing in *particular Cases*, yet the *Power*
it self not being *declar'd* as a *Doctrinal Point* ; and the
Decrees relating only to matter of *Discipline* and *Government*, it comes short of being an *Article* of our
Faith, and all that in your *Answer* depends on it, falls
to the Ground. I have no place here to give you a
distinct

distinct account of the several matters treated of in
Councils, and of the difference between Decrees of
Faith, and *others* which are not so; yet because you
seem to require some satisfaction in these Points, I remit you to such Authors, who treat of them at large,
and most particularly the *Considerations upon the Council of Trent*, *Canus*, *Bellarmine* and others. This
that I have here said may be sufficient to evince, that
in my declaring the *deposing Power* to be *no Article of
Faith*, I have not follow'd my own Private Opinion,
or meerly the *number* of Authors, but rather the sense
of the *whole Church, Councils, and Popes* themselves,
who plainly enough own this, in letting so many open
and Positive Assertors of the *no-deposing Power*, to
pass without any Censure of *Heresie* : It being certain
that, were this Doctrine any *Article* of our *Faith*, as
likewise that mention'd in the preceding Paragraph,
of the *Popes Personal Infallibility*, the obstinate Op-
posers of them would no more escape without *that
brand*, than those that deny *other Articles* of our
Faith, as *Purgatory* and *Transubstantiation*.

These Instances I look upon as the most Principal
throughout your whole *Reply*, because in them you
have made use of a *Medium* directly opposit to the *Intent* of my Book, and which if it had been effectual,
would have shew'd, that I have not Represented the
Faith of the *Papist* according to the *Rule* of approv'd
General Councils, as I pretend; but rather according
to my own private apprehension or Opinion; which
I confess would have been a *full Answer* to it as to such
particulars. But how far you have fail'd of your
endeavours even in this Point, I leave now to the
Prudent Considerer to judge. But the way you take
in

in all other Parts of your Book, feems to me not to anfwer your defign, nor to agree with the *Title* of it. For whereas I undertake to propofe the *Faith* of a *Roman Catholick*, as he is really taught to believe in Conformity to the Definitions of Oecumenical Councils: Bating thofe Points I have already fpoke to, in your *Anfwer*,

You either own the Doctrine, to be the eftablifh'd Belief of *your Church*, as in part that of the *Power* of *Prieftly Abfolution,Confeffion*, of due veneration to the *Relicks* of *Saints*, of *Merit*, of *Satisfaction*, of the *Authority* of the *Church*, of *General Councils*, &c.

Or you fhew the Doctrine I have deliver'd, not to be the Faith of our Church, by appealing from the Definitions of our *Councils*, and *fenfe* of our *Church*, to fome expreffions found in Old *Mafs-books*, *Rituals* &c. as if this were a ferious way of *truly Reprefenting* the Doctrines of the *Church* of *Rome*. Can any *Religion* ftand this *Teft*? Will not many Expreffions in all forts of *Prayers, Preaching,*and *Devotions*, if feparate from the *fenfe* of the *Church*, prove unjuftifiable and Ridiculous? Let but an *Atheift* take this liberty even with the *Scripture* it felf, and thus feparate infinite number of expreffions there, and fee what will be prefently the colour of *all Religion*, and whether *Chriftianity* will be better than *Turcifm*: And efpecially whether the *allow'd Pfalms* in *Meeter* will prove the devotion of men of *fence* and *reafon*, tho all may be reconcileable to Piety and Religion, if taken in the *fenfe* of the *Church*.

Or you appeal again from the Declarations of our Councils, and fenfe of our Church to fome *external Action*, as in cafe of refpect fhewn to *Images* and

pag. 34, 35.

B 2 *Saints,*

pag. 21.

Saints, upon which from our *external* Adoration, by *construction of the Fact,* viz. *kneeling, bowing,* &c. you are willing to conclude us guilty of Idolatry : As if a true judgment could be made of *these Actions,* without respect to the *Intention* of the *Church,* that directs them , and of the *Person,* that does them. As if they were not in themselves *Indifferent,* and capable of being paid to *God,* or to *Men.* Or as if your measures being follow'd, *Abigail* ought not to come in, and share with us in our *constructive Idolatry,* because

1 Sam. 25. 24. *she fell before* David *on her face, and bow'd her self to*

Jof. 5. 14. *the ground, and fell at his feet. Joshua* likewise, because he *fell on his face to the earth, and did worship the Angel.* And as many who on their knees pay their respects to the *King* and *bow* before him : As likewise all the Beggers in *Lincolns-Inn* fields, who on their knees, with their hands lifted up, ask an alms of Passers-by : Must not all these by *construction of Fact* come into the list of your *Idolaters?*

Or finally, not being willing the Doctrine should pass for *ours,* in the form I have stated it, you appeal again from our *Councils* and *Sense* of the *Church,* which I follow, to the Sentiments of some of our own *Private Authors,* and so you come often with, this *French Author* says this, *Vives* says that, *Wicelius* says another thing, and *Lessius* another; by this method endeavouring to convince your Reader, that the *Belief* of a *Papist,* is much different from what I have represented it. But Sir, this way may do well enough with the unwary; but it ill suits with what you pretend. The Frontis piece of your Book puts us upon expecting *The Doctrines and Practices of the Church of Rome truly Represented.* And when

we

we come to perufe it, we find feveral Doctrines propos'd, but without any Authority of *Church* or *Councils*, but *this Author fays this*, and *that Author fays
that* ; as if the Senfe of every *Author*, were immediately the Doctrine ; of our *Church*. The *Church*
fpeaks to us in her *approv'd General Councils* , and
from them you might have *truly Reprefented* her *Belief* and *Doctrine* but from *particular Authors*, fome
of which may Write upon a Pique, others upon a Paffion, others upon fome other Biafs, nothing more
can be Collected befides their *own Opinion*, and with
underftanding Men it paffes for no more. So that
nothing can be more unjuftifiable, than to make a
Collection of *private* Mens fentiments, and obtrude
them for the *truly Reprefenting* the Doctrine of the
Church in whofe Communion they are. And this is
not the Cafe of *our Church* alone, there's no *Church*
or Congregation in the World will ftand this Teft.
And if it come a little home to you, it may be you
will be more fenfible of this truth. For altho you feem
to maintain in your *Anfwer*, that *good works of juftified* p. 57.
Perfons are not Free ; yet tis not juft, *this Doctrine*
fhould be immediately charg'd for the *Belief* of *your
Church*. Altho Mr. *Thorndike* feems to allow *Prayers for
the Dead*, yet neither from him are we to take a *true
reprefentation* of the *Doctrin* of *his Church*. Tho a worthy
Divine declares, *that in cafe a Popifh* Julian *indeed fhould* pag. 152.
*Reign over us, he fhould Believe him uncapable of Repen-
tance, and upon that fuppofition fhould be tempted to pray
for his Deftruction* ; yet would it not be honeft hence to
blacken *his Church* with this Dif-loyal Principle, as if
fhe allowed her *Members*, tho not to Fight againft, yet
to *Pray for the Deftruction* of *fuch a Prince*. The like
may

may be said of *King James* the *First* his holding Chrift to be *truly prefent* in the *Sacrament*, and there alfo to be truly ador'd, maintaining in his Epiftle to Cardinal *Perron* the Doctrine of the *Real Prefence* to be the Doctrine of the Church of *England;* and again what the aforefaid Mr. *Thorndike* delivers of the fame *Real Prefence* and *Adoration* of Chrift in the *Eucharift*, practis'd in the Ancient Church from the beginning; and thereupon owning the *Euchariftical Sacrifice* to be truely the *Sacrifice* of Chrift upon the *Crofs*, in as much as the Body and Blood of Chrift are contain'd in them ; and then farther adding, that the Sacrifice of the Crofs being neceffarily Propitiatory and Impetratory both, it cannot be denied, that the Sacrament of the *Eucharift*, in as much as it is the fame Sacrifice of Chrift upon the Crofs, is alfo both Propitiatory and Impetratory. Will you give me leave from hence to inferr; that becaufe thefe are the fentiments of fuch Eminent Perfons in the Communion of the *Church* of *England*, that therefore they are the Doctrine of that Church, I fuppofe you will not ; and therefore in the *true Reprefentation* of the Doctrine of yours or our Chuch, I fuppofe, you will eafily grant, that no appeal ought to be made to fuch *Private Authors* ; but the Undertaker is oblig'd to keep clofe to the *fenfe* of either *Church*, declar'd in their *Councils* and *Decrees*, and as explicated by their Authority : And as far as you have effectually prov'd this againft what I have reprefented for the Faith of a *Papift*, fo fo far will I allow you have given me a *juft Anfwer* ; And as much as you fail of this, fo much you come fhort of what you undertake, which I recommend to your own perufal to examine.

Fpil. L. 3. c. 5.

But

But for any of thefe ways they are infignificant to your defign, and deferve not to ftand under the Title of an *Anfwer*. For how does your acknowledging our Doctrine to be yours: your producing fome broken Expreffions out of *Mafs-Books*, your putting Objections from *external Actions*, from *private Authors*, or your *own Opinion*, any ways prove, that the Faith of a *Papift*, as I have reprefented it, is not according to the Council of *Trent*, and what really he is bound, as a *Papift*, to *Believe?* And yet this is the thing you ought to have prov'd, to make good your *Title*. But inftead of this, you generally let your Reader underftand, that I have indeed ftated the matter aright, and only tell him, that you have fomething to fay againft the Doctrine, and do not like it. But your faying I hope (or if it could be proving) that Catholicks do not do well to Believe, as I *Reprefent*, is no Argument to prove that I do not *Reprefent well*. This as to the Reprefenting the Doctrine of our Church.

' I fhould fay fomething to your concluding Argument which comes fo home (*p.* 14.) I allow it feems, the *Orders of the Supream Paftor are to be obey'd, whether he be Infallible or no*. I confefs likewife in another place, that *fome Popes have own'd the Depofing Doctrine, and Acted according to it*. And here you infer, Therefore the *Papifts* are bound by the Doctrine of their Church to Act, when the Popes fhall require it, according to the Depofing Power. And does this *bring the matter home?* Why then Sir, you muft ee'n give me leave to make another inference: That, What brings the matter home is nothing but an ordinary piece of Sophiftry, and let the Reader judge.

judge. The Reprefenter (*p.* 42.) fpeaking of the Popes Authority, fays, that as in any Civil Govern-ment, the Sentence of the Supream Judge or Higheft Tribunal is to be Obey'd, thô there be no affurance of Infallibility or Divine Protection from Error or Miftake: So is he taught fhould be done to the Orders of the Supream Paftor, whetherhe be Infallible or no.

Where a Parallel is made between the Orders of *Popes* and *Civil Powers*, as to the *Obedience* due to them from their *Subjects*. Now Sir, if it be your Opinion that this Authority and Power in *thefe Supream* Governours is fo *Abfolute* and *Unconfin'd*, that like to *God* himfelf there can be no juft exception made to any of their *Actions* or *Decrees*, whatfoever they be: then indeed your reafoning Anfwers your intent. But if the Cafe be poffible, that thefe may *fo* Act or Command, that the *not-following* or *not-obeying* in Inferiors may be *no Crime*; then you come but fhort of home, and prove juft nothing. Now change but the *matter* of your Argument, and fee how far it goes. The Orders of a *Prince*, being Supream Governour, are to be Obey'd, whether he be Infallible or no: But *fome* Princes have done *thus* and *thus*; therefore the People by the Law are bound to Act *fo* and *fo*: Does this hold in *every* Action or Order of a Prince, without *Limit* or *Exception*? Tho a Prince be to be obey'd, yet it follows not that his Word is the Law? So that whofoever takes this for a concluding Argument, muft neither underftand *Law* nor *Logick*.

I need not put the Reader in mind, how often you make your digreffions amongft the *School-men*, and leave not fcouting among them, till you have loft the matter in hand: And difpute about their *Opinions*, in-ftead

Head of matter of *Faith*; how in the Point of *difpen-*
fations, where we fpeak of the *Moral Law*; and affert the *Pope* cannot difpenfe with it, as give leave to
break the *Commandments*, to *lye or for-fwear* : You
fhew your learning, in proving he can difpenfe
with other *Laws* and *Pofitive Inftitutions*, a thing
fcarce to be doubted of, and nothing to our purpofe.
I'le fay nothing of the admirable clofe of Your Chap-
ter of *Difpenfations*, in which, tho you have not produc'd one proof of *Difpenfations*, for *lying* or *for*
fwearing being allow'd in our Church on any account
whatfoever, you yet give this affurance to your Reader; *We know this Difpenfing Power is to be kept up as a*
great Myftery, and not to be made ufe of, but upon weigh-
ty and urgent Caufes — as their Doctrines declare.
Where certainly one proof of the *Who*, the *Where*
and the *When*, had been much more Satisfactory, than
the Pofitive *We know*, and *Their Doctrines declare* :
For tho many are willing to take this upon truft, yet
it would have gone farther, if you had prov'd it down
right, without taking Sanctuary in a *Myftery*. I'le
pafs by your dexterity wherewith you have manag'd
the Hiftory of St. *Perpetua* in the Chap. of *Purgatory* :
Where after you have difguis'd it to your purpofe in
the Relation, and drol'd the *Vifion* of a *Martyr*, and
fo efteem'd by St. *Auguftin*, into a young Ladies
Dream, you at laft fet it forth for the *Foundation* of
our Churches Doctrine, and would perfwade your
Reader, that Our Tenent of *Purgatory* is *built* upon
it; when 'tis us'd by me for no more, than a *Margi-*
nal Citation, amongft feveral others : And yet this is
our *Foundation*, and our Doctrine is *built* on it :
Here I fear, you had forgot your promife made in the

pag. 117.

C   begin-

pag. 9.

beginning of being *fincere*, and ufing no *Tricks*. But I forbear;

And will only conclude, that if you have *truly re-prefented the Doctrines of the Church of Rome*, I would as foon be a *Turk* as *your Papift*; whofe character you have drawn at large throughout your Book, and *in little* in pag, 161. Which, however you may call *truly reprefenting,* I can look upon no better than *truly Mif-reprefenting.* And by what I fee, I think I might with as good reafon go to a *Pharifee*, to be inform'd of *Chrift*, and receive the Character of a *Chriftian* from a *Mahometan*; as come to *you*, to know what a *Papift* is, what his *Belief* and *Doctrine.* Neither do I wonder, that you come thus wide of what you pretend to : The method you take, would bring a Scandal even upon the *Apoftles* themfelves, and render the *Church* of thofe purer times, of the fame colour with *ours.* Obferve but the *fame,* in drawing the Features of *your own Church*, and then tell me whether this be the way of *truely reprefenting.* If a man were but to bring into publick your *School-debates*, the *differing Opinions* of your own Authors, concerning the *Scriptures, Predeftination, Freewill,* the *Authority* of the *Church*, the *Reformation, Traditions*, &c. all expreffions of *Sermons, Prayers,* &c. and out of thefe, and all others of this kind, pick out and patch up a *Religion* according to the beft contrivance of the Undertaker, and then fhew it forth to the world, do you think, this would be *yours truly reprefented?* Why then muft fuch another *Jumble* as this be expofed to the World for *ours?* If you'l let your Flock fee what our Religion is, fend them to the *Council* of *Trent*, the *Catechifm ad*

ad Parochos ; this wee'l own and ſtand by ;
But for you to pick here a bit and there a bit, to patch
as you pleaſe, to make your Inferences and Applica-
tions at pleaſure, and then to tell your Reader, theſe
are the Doctrines of the *Church of Rome truly Repre-*
ſented; this is to abuſe the World and your ſelves,
and to render us Infamous for principles which are
nothing of *our Religion.* And in Caſe you do not
judge what I have here ſaid ſufficient to convince you,
that the *Faith*, as I have *Repreſented* it, is really the
Faith of a *Papiſt*, I'le be content all theſe Reaſons at
preſent paſs for nought; and that the deciſion of this
whole affair depend upon an *Experience.* Do but
you, (or any Friend for you) give your Aſſent to thoſe
Articles of Faith, in the very form and manner, as
I have ſtated them, in the Character of the *Papiſt*
Repreſented; and if upon requeſt, you are not ad-
mitted into the Communion of the *Roman Catholicks*,
and own'd to Believe *aright* in all thoſe Points, I'le
then Confeſs, that I have abus'd the World, that my
Repreſenting is *Miſ-repreſenting* the Faith of a *Papiſt*,
and that my deſign has been not to undeceive, but to
deceive the People. But if on the contrary it ſhall
appear, that the Faith, as I have Repreſented it, is
the approv'd Doctrine of that Church, and ſufficient
for any one to be receiv'd a Member of it, I may
then juſtly renew my Complaint of its being *Miſ-re-*
preſented, that the Religion of the Papiſt is nothing
like what 'tis commonly render'd; and that 'tis a hard
fate, that the Profeſſors of it ſhould be ſo injur'd in
their Reputation, and by this means become ſo *Odious*,
that even amongſt Fellow-Chriſtians , *Atheiſts* and
Jews, ſhall be tolerated with leſs regret than they.

F I N I S.